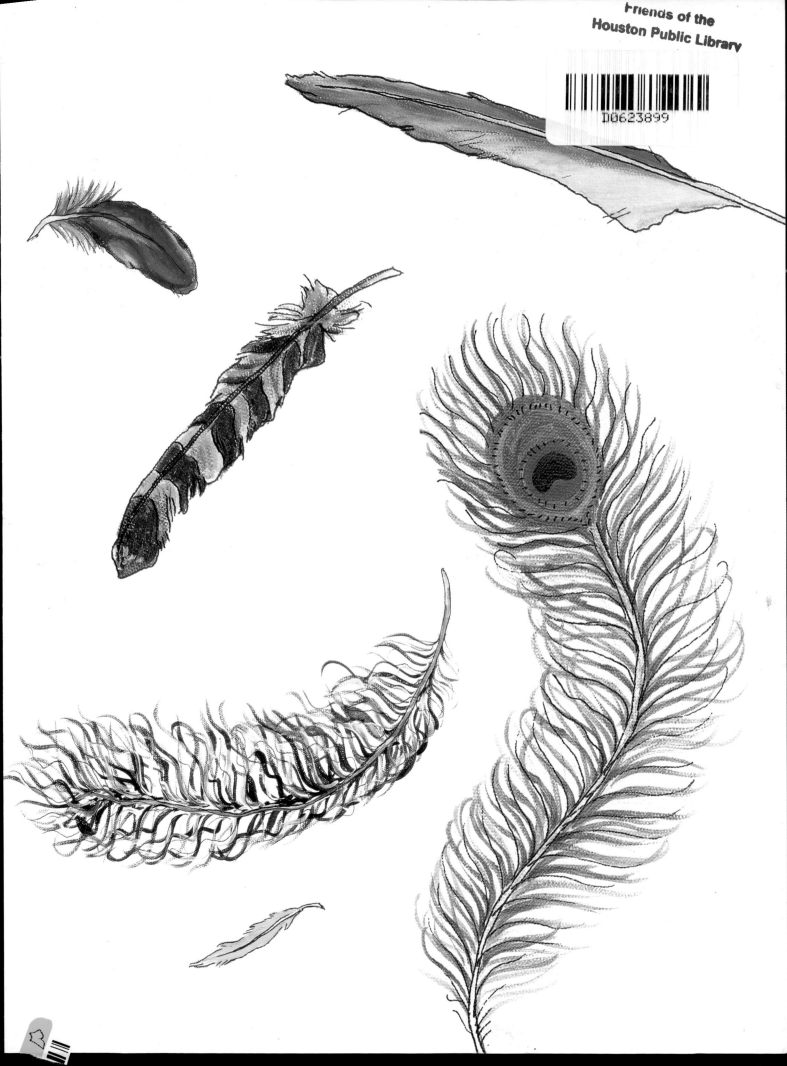

All net profits from this book will be donated to
charitable organizations, with a gentle preference towards
people with my husband's disease – multiple sclerosis.

Vanita Oelschlager

Acknowledgements

Many Thanks to:

Robin Hegan

Jennie Levy Smith

Kurt Landefeld

Paul Royer

Larry Chilnick

Mike Blanc

Sheila Tarr

Cinda Dehner

Kristin Johnston

Birds of a Feather
VanitaBooks, LLC
All rights reserved.
© 2009 VanitaBooks, LLC
No part of this book may be reproduced, stored in retrieval systems, or transmitted in any form or
through methods including electronic photocopying, online download, or any other system now known
or hereafter invented – except by reviewers, who may quote brief passages in a review to be printed in a
newspaper or print or online publication – without express written permission from VanitaBooks, LLC.
Text by Vanita Oelschlager.
Illustrations by Robin Hegan.
Design by Jennie Levy Smith,
Trio Design & Marketing Communications Inc.
Printed in China.
ISBN 978-0-9800162-8-4

www.VanitaBooks.com

written by **Vanita Oelschlager** *illustrated by* **Robin Hegan**

This book is dedicated with love to:
All my grandchildren
Who are 'the salt of the earth'
Vanita Oelschlager

This book is dedicated to:
My Snickle-Pickles
Robin Hegan

Birds of a Feather

a book of **idioms** *and* **silly pictures**

Goosebumps

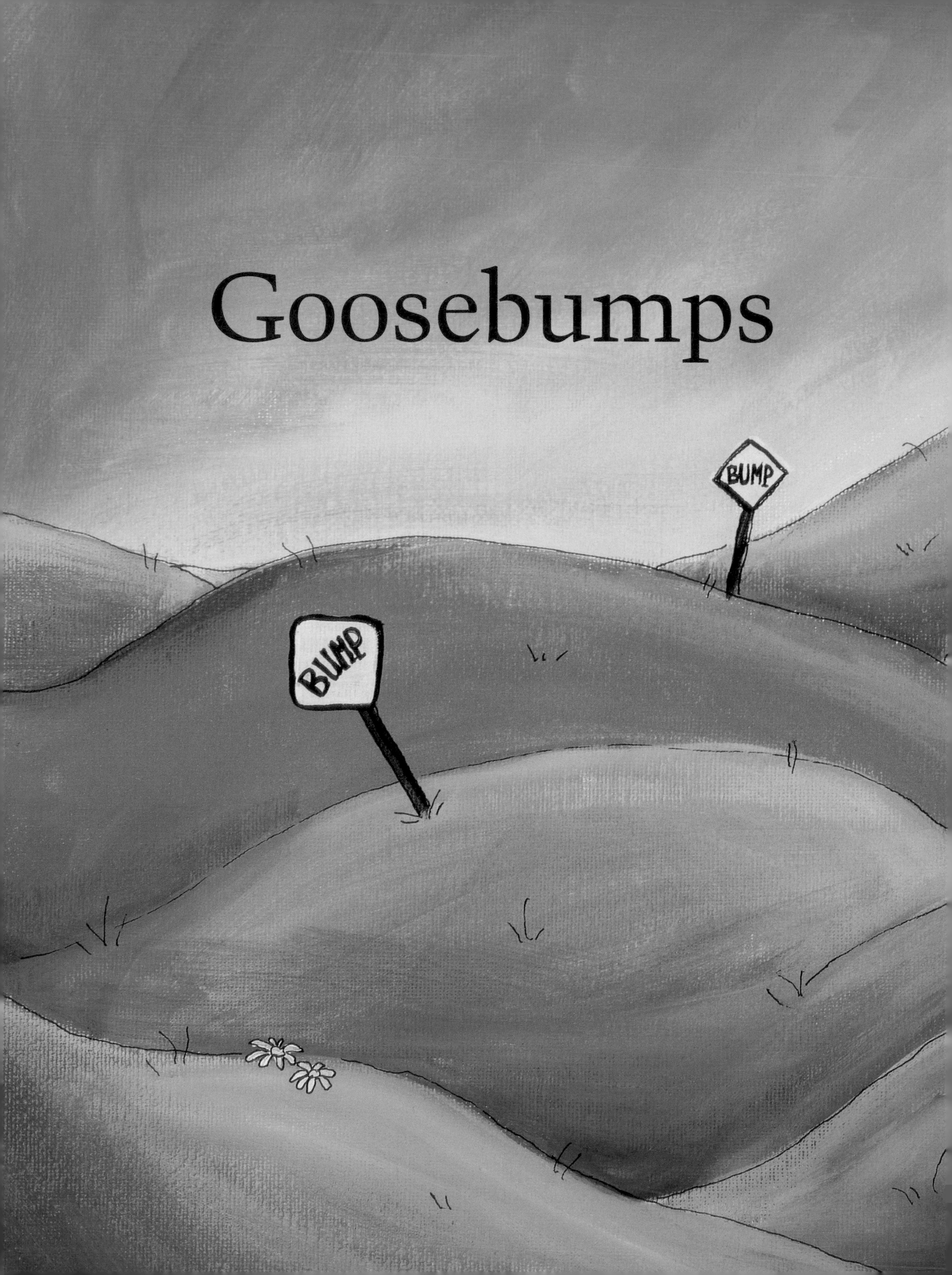

Goosebumps are the little bumps on your skin when you feel cold or creepy.

"She shivered with **goosebumps** when she forgot her coat."

Raining cats and dogs

A very loud and heavy rain storm.

"Don't go outside now. It's raining cats and dogs."

Bull in a china shop

You are clumsy when you
should be careful.

"You have knocked over three things.
You are like a *bull in a china shop*."

Birds of a feather flock together

Animals and people are found among their own kind.

"Those twins are birds of a feather."

Bright eyed and bushy tailed

If someone is *bright eyed and bushy tailed*, they are fully awake and ready to go.

"Would you look at him this morning? He just woke up and he's already *bright eyed and bushy tailed*."

Bring home the bacon

The person who *brings home the bacon* is the person who earns the money that the family lives on.

"In our family, my dad *brings home the bacon*."

"Will you look at that? Look what the cat dragged in."

This idiom is used when someone arrives somewhere looking a mess and maybe even smelling bad.

Look what the cat dragged in

Snug as a bug in a rug

You are snuggled in and are very comfortable and safe.

"He was snug as a bug in a rug, curled up in his chair with his blanket."

This means you are not young anymore.
"Your grandma is *no spring chicken*."

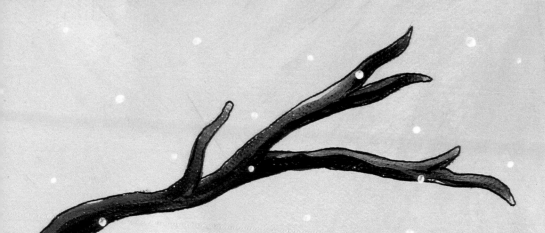

No spring chicken

Butterflies in
your stomach

The feeling you get in your stomach when you are nervous or afraid.

"She had **butterflies in her stomach** as she walked onto the stage."

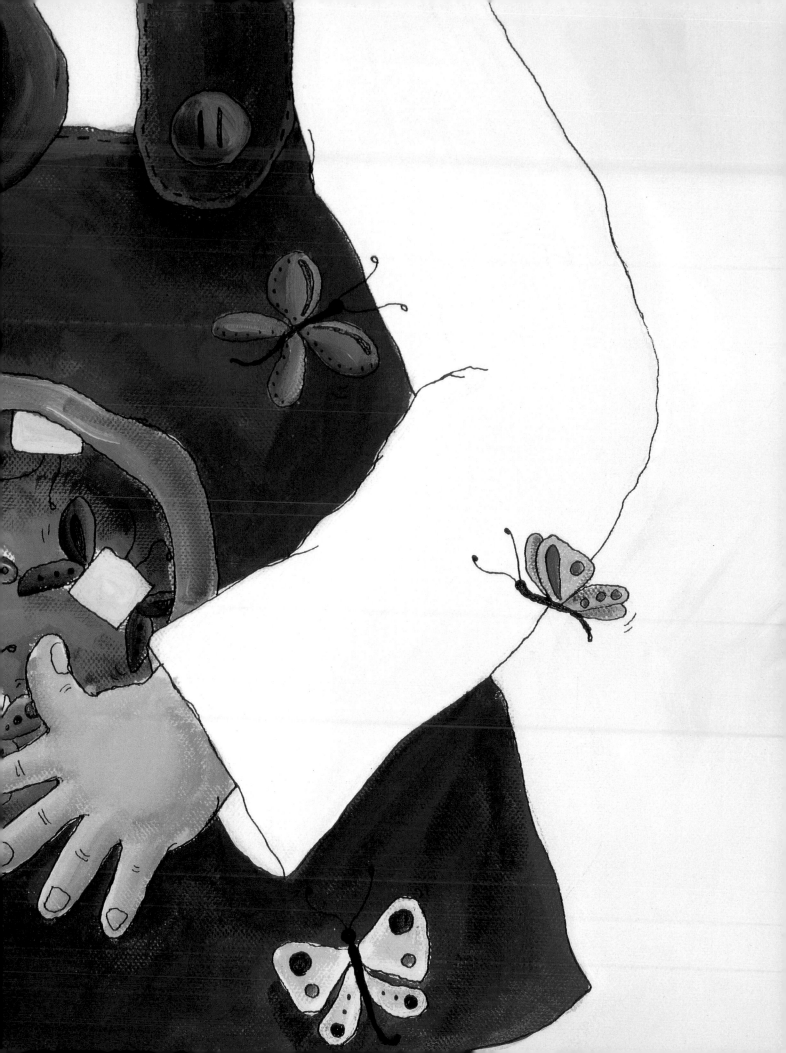

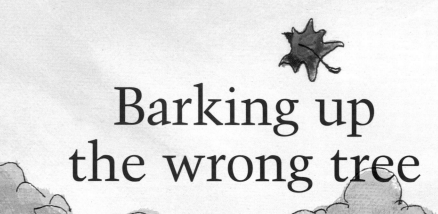

Barking up
the wrong tree

This means you make a mistake in something you are trying to do.

"You'll never find the answer there. You're barking up the wrong tree."

A wild goose chase

"There he goes again on another wild goose chase."

This is something you do that is a waste of time, or chase after that can't be caught. (Farm geese can't fly and are more easily caught – wild geese can always fly beyond reach.)

Hogwash

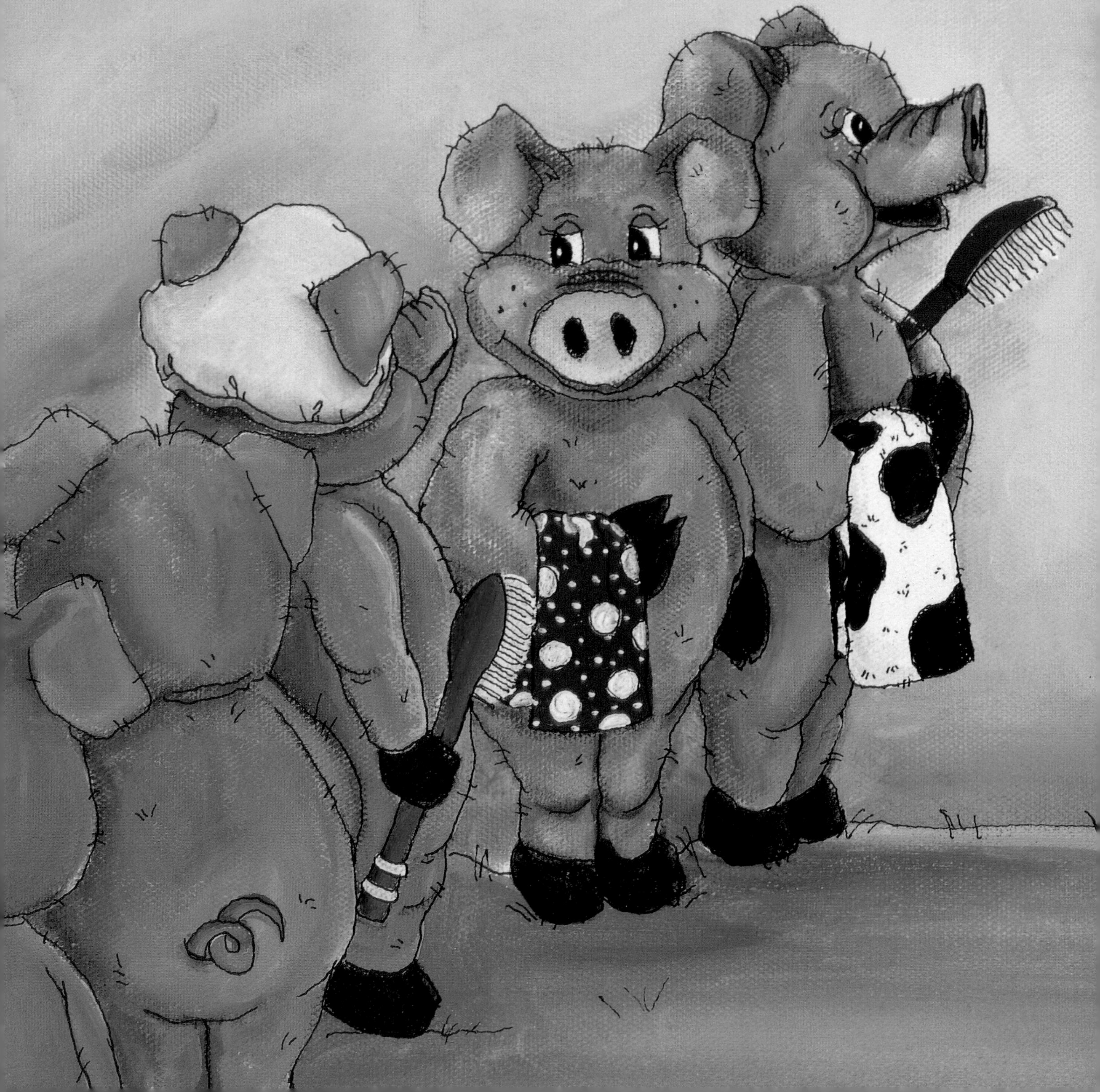

If something you say or write is not true, or worthless, it is hogwash.

"That is not true. It is just hogwash."

Ants in
your pants

If you have *ants in your pants* you are excited and squirmy and can't sit still.

"Would you please sit still? You act like you have ants in your pants."

Let the cat out of the bag

To share a secret that wasn't supposed to be shared.

"That was a secret and you let the cat out of the bag."

What are idioms?

Every language has idioms, and the English language has thousands of them. You cannot understand them because the group of words together has little, often nothing, to do with the meanings of the words taken one by one.

For instance, to **bark up the wrong tree** means to have the wrong idea about something. Today, the phrase has nothing to do with a dog or a tree, but hundreds of years ago, it actually did.

In order to understand a language, you must know what the idioms in that language mean. If you try to figure out the meaning of the idiom word by word you're likely to get nowhere – you will get befuddled or confused. You have to know the 'hidden' meaning.

I am going to show you the 'hidden' meaning of one idiom. Maybe you can find out the 'hidden' meaning of some other idioms in this book. Idioms show a language's sense of humor; they're your language's ticklish spots so learning them can be lots of fun. I hope you'll enjoy them as much as we do.

Bark up the wrong tree.

Here is the 'hidden' meaning. During colonial times in America, raccoon hunting was a popular sport. Trained dogs would chase a raccoon up a tree and bark furiously at the base until the hunter came. Sometimes a raccoon could escape to the branches of another tree, and another, getting away and leaving the dog **barking up the wrong tree**.

Like two peas in a pod

Vanita Oelschlager is a wife, mother, grandmother, former teacher, caregiver, author, and poet. She was named "Writer in Residence" for the Literacy Program at The University of Akron in 2007. She is a graduate of Mount Union College, Alliance, Ohio, where she is currently a member of the Board of Trustees.

Robin Hegan grew up in the Laurel Mountains of Pennsylvania where imagination took her and her childhood friends on many great adventures. After graduating from The Pennsylvania State University with a degree in Integrative Arts, Robin resided in Ohio for several years until she and her husband, Matt, decided to return to the mountains of Pennsylvania to raise their children. Robin's illustrations can also be seen in *My Grampy Can't Walk* and *Mother Goose Other Goose*. To find out more about Robin, visit www.robinhegan.com.

When two people are alike in some ways.

"The author and the illustrator are *like two peas in a pod*. They both like to make books for children to enjoy."

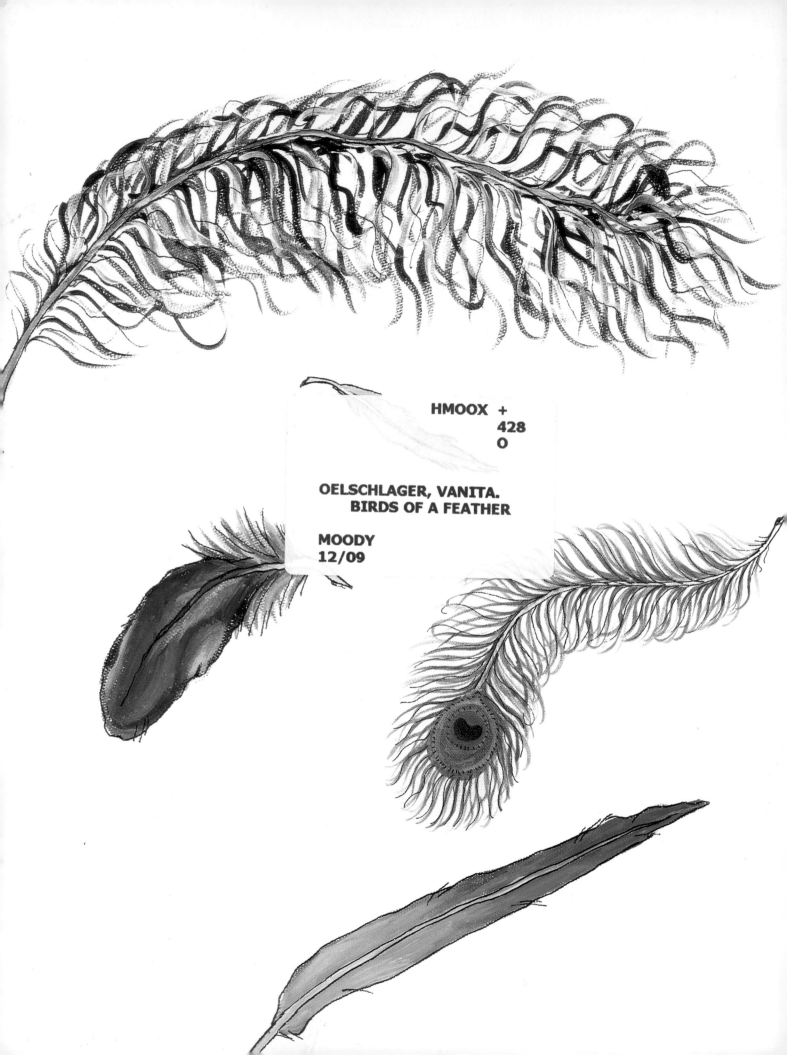

HMOOX +
428
O

OELSCHLAGER, VANITA.
BIRDS OF A FEATHER

MOODY
12/09